MUSLIMA COACHING WIFE TIPS SERIES

SECRETS OF SUCCESSFUL MUSLIM WIVES

By Naielah Ackbarali

muslima
coaching

This book is copyrighted and under the sole ownership of MuslimaCoaching.com. No part of this book can be copied, reproduced, distributed, or shared in any form or by any means without prior permission from MuslimaCoaching.com.

© Muslima Coaching, 2019.

All Rights Reserved.

*Good women are for good men,
and good men for good women.*

(Qur'an 24:26)

CONTENTS

THE UNSPOKEN SECRET   1

PART 1: MENTAL FOCUS   9

◆ Three Questions That Successful Wives Ask

PART 2: EMOTIONAL INTELLIGENCE   29

◆ Three Habits That Define Successful Wives

PART 3: INTERNAL RESOLVE   49

◆ Three Commitments That Successful Wives Make

ABOUT THE AUTHOR   67

THE UNSPOKEN SECRET

Can you keep a secret?

I mean a really BIG secret.

Okay, I trust that you won't disappoint me. Here we go:

Successful marriages do exist…

AND their successful tactics can be practiced by almost anyone.

I'm serious. Put aside what you've heard and the depressing statistics that came with it. This story line is only going to get juicier with each page turn.

I understand why it may seem hard to believe. It seems like every week we hear about a new divorce.

Couples who we thought were sure to be winners because they were married for 'x' amount of years and with 'x' number of children are suddenly breaking up and moving on.

While these individuals may be entering a new stage in life, little do they know that their separation has left us feeling disappointed and sad.

So much that we may even start to become curious about what occurred in their marriage, ponder over what will happen to their children, and deliberate about whose marriage will be next.

Like you, I've sailed in the same boat of wandering daydreams, thinking good marriages were the next extinct species on planet Earth.

But when I became a marriage coach, things changed. Now, I get a sneak peek into the reality of people's marriages all the time and I want to share the truth.

Yes, there are struggling marriages. But what's often overlooked is that there are good marriages too – really good ones. However, the catch is that they are becoming fewer and fewer.

This is why I've decided to hunt down Muslim women who are in good marriages, question their wife techniques, and summarize them for you.

Yet, we need to come to an agreement before I spill the beans.

Rather than preoccupying ourselves with bad stories and negative emotions, let's change our track of thought and seize the opportunity to benefit.

How about personally reflecting about our own marriages instead?

Are we in a blissful marriage?

Are we actively making the consistent moves to better our relationship?

Are we conscious of how much our daily marital choices will play a toll on the quality of our children's future marriages?

> RATHER THAN PREOCCUPYING OURSELVES WITH BAD STORIES AND NEGATIVE EMOTIONS, LET'S CHANGE OUR TRACK OF THOUGHT AND SEIZE THE OPPORTUNITY TO BENEFIT.

What I've found over the years of speaking with various Muslim women is that successful wives astonishingly use the same successful tactics.

I want to share how these women make their marriages loving, peaceful, and emotionally safe.

Successful Muslim wives essentially resort to a combination of mental, emotional, and heart-centered tactics.

The best part about it all is that these tactics are NOT difficult to carry out – meaning that you, me, and any Muslim wife can use them too!

These tactics are proven to work, providing that we are sincere in our desire to make our marriage pleasing for the sake of Allah Most High.

All ears?! Good! Because I really want to share what I've discovered.

So, lean in and listen to what love secrets have been unlocked.

Reflection Exercise

Take a moment to reflect about your own marriage. Are you happy with your marriage? Why or why not?

_____
_____
_____
_____
_____
_____
_____
_____
_____
_____
_____
_____
_____

PART 1: MENTAL FOCUS

THREE QUESTIONS THAT SUCCESSFUL WIVES ASK

What many people fail to realize is that most marriage problems are actually first born from what is occurring in our minds.

Our thoughts play a huge role in forming our perspectives about people, and our judgement will shape the way that we react and respond to others, including our 'lucky' husband.

Feeling upset about our marriage very much boils down to our perspective and our attitude – how we interpret the events occurring in our relationship.

Successful wives protect the longevity of their marriages by monitoring their thoughts with three key questions.

QUESTION #1: HOW CAN I SEE HIS SIDE IN THIS?

Sometimes, the way we interpret events hurts us more than what actually happened.

When we stick to the facts, we're less likely to let our emotions drive us.

On the other hand, when we only think about how we've been wronged, then we're setting ourselves up for relationship failure.

That lurking thought that drives us to think that we've been mistreated can become possessive.

If we permit it to gain influence, it can lead us to unfairly judge our husband's intentions and motives.

As our upset and anger intensifies, our ability to hold a good opinion of him soon goes out the window.

We may even label our husband as selfish, incompetent, cheap, mean, inconsiderate, or the like.

However, what if it's not true?

What if our husband is actually not the bad guy that we sometimes envision him to be?

What if he has a good reason for doing what he did?

What if we're only focusing on certain details and we're not seeing the entire picture?

PART 1: MENTAL FOCUS

It's very hard to form an accurate judgement about someone when we do not hear all parts of the story.

Even more so, whenever our hearts are involved in the matter, it becomes doubly challenging to assume the role of a fair judge.

Allah Most High says: "O ye who believe! Avoid suspicion as much (as possible): for suspicion in some cases is a sin." (Qur'an 49:12)

Successful Muslim wives give their husbands the benefit of the doubt.

It does not mean that they never experience bad thoughts about their husbands. They do, but it's short-lived.

So, how do they pop the angry pressure building up in their mental balloon?

Simple.

They stop feeding the negativity felt towards their husbands' behavior by satiating their hearts with this wholesome question:

"How can I see his side in this?"

When we give our husband the benefit of the doubt, the good thoughts about him suddenly jump out of the bushes and beat the living daylights out of our negativity.

> *Aisha was constantly bothered by her husband's recent life decisions. In his early thirties, he decided to change his career track and move to another country.*
>
> *Even though it forced her to start budgeting after living a more financially secure life, she was supportive. But as time passed, the couple found themselves fighting more than usual, especially in front of their young son.*
>
> *It seemed like her husband was only thinking of himself and not the well-being of the entire family. Every time Aisha dwelled on the thought that her husband was selfish, her anger raged.*
>
> *Yet, whenever she chose to remember that her husband was a good man at heart and that he would not purposely ignore her needs, she felt different. And this change*

PART 1: MENTAL FOCUS

of heart made her act differently towards him too.

Within days after changing her focus, her husband was inviting her to watch the sun rise on the rooftop and buying her sweet gifts.

Once she realized the perks of this route, Aisha promised herself that she would work towards focusing more on her husband's good qualities. As a result, the couple's marriage took a turn for the better.

The moral of the story is that successful Muslim wives refuse to believe that their husband intended to hurt them, and they look for a more reasonable explanation instead.

For example:

"He probably doesn't know that it hurt me."

"I can understand why he did that if I put myself in his shoes."

"If I'm honest, I can see how I'm at fault too and my comments probably influenced his reaction."

By asking this key question, anger subdues, clarity returns, and the road to mending hearts is opened.

> **QUESTION #2: DOES IT REALLY MATTER IN THE LONG-RUN?**

So maybe he forgot to pay the phone bill on time this month.

He also didn't take out the trash today when he was reminded twice.

In fact, he hasn't fixed the door that's still surviving off of one hinge for the past month!

It's ridiculous to try to see our husband's side when his behavior reflects sheer irresponsibility and negligence on his part.

The truth is that we all have situations when our husband does things – or forgets to do things – that make us doubt his credibility as a provider, protector, and father.

He could definitely be prioritizing his time in the way that he thinks is best, but sometimes his ranking method can get quite annoying.

This is why successful Muslim wives ask themselves:

"Does it really matter in the long-run?"

If it boils down to being right or wrong, we could be in the right, but is our overemphasizing this to our husband going to give us the marriage of our dreams?

Will it annoy our husband or hurt our friendship?

Will it make our husband feel nagged, put down, or defensive?

If the majority of our answers lean towards something that will harm our marriage, then we must seriously consider if it's worth the trouble.

It is a common tendency for humans to focus on what is going wrong instead of what is going right, but it is counterproductive in a long-term relationship.

The Prophet (Allah bless him and give him peace) said, "Whoever conceals the faults of a Muslim, Allah will conceal his faults in this world and in the Hereafter." (Muslim)

A marriage is a union of two imperfect beings.

IT IS A COMMON TENDENCY FOR HUMANS TO FOCUS ON WHAT IS GOING WRONG INSTEAD OF WHAT IS GOING RIGHT, BUT IT IS COUNTERPRODUCTIVE IN A LONG-TERM RELATIONSHIP.

Constantly nitpicking our husband's bad traits blinds us from the blessings raining down in our

PART 1: MENTAL FOCUS

lives, and it can also be an act of ingratitude towards Allah Most High for what He is giving us.

Successful Muslim wives can gauge what is worth fighting for and what is not. After trial and error, they become comfortable with their husband's imperfections because they know that these issues are minor and will not matter tomorrow, a month later, a year from now, or even five years from today!

> *Iman was irritated at her husband's lack of attention towards helping keep the house tidy. It seemed like almost every day she was picking up his dirty pairs of socks from all corners of the house.*
>
> *"Why can't he just remember to put them in the laundry basket?" she would think to herself. She even made the effort to remind him on several occasions, but her husband kept forgetting to do it.*
>
> *One day he would remember, and then the next day it was if he had amnesia about the whole affair.*

Within time, Iman found herself getting offended at the sight of his socks freely lying around the house like they were at a fancy vacation spa. She interpreted her husband's inattentiveness to mean that he didn't care about her efforts to maintain the house's clean appearance.

Iman knew that her husband worked crazy hours to provide a good life for her. He was a generous and caring man. He was probably too tired to remember to put his socks away or perhaps consumed with more important work matters.

Even so, Iman's thoughts about her husband's reasons for being remiss drove her wild and they would overpower her honest attempts to form a good opinion of him, which caused her to feel distant from her husband at times.

One day a good friend said to her, "Is it really something to dwell over? Just help him out and pick them up."

Eureka! In that moment, she realized that didn't have to make a big deal out of it. Iman felt like something heavy had been lifted off of her. The negativity that her thoughts produced just wasn't worth it.

By weighing out the pros and cons about what is aggravating us, we learn what issues are truly important and what things can be put on hold for the time being.

We develop the patience to endure a lifelong relationship.

We begin to empathize with other people's circumstances instead of only selfishly focusing on what we want from the other person.

All of this gives us a chance to feel that love and admiration once again for our dear hubby.

QUESTION #3: WHAT DO I NEED RIGHT NOW TO MAKE MYSELF HAPPY?

As much as it may be tempting to point all fingers possible at our husband for making us unhappy, the reality is that happiness is a personal choice.

The Prophet (Allah bless him and give him peace) said, "How excellent is the affair of the believer! Verily, there is good for him in everything and this applies only to the believer. If prosperity comes to him, he is thankful, and if adversity falls on him, he perseveres patiently and that is better for him." (Muslim)

Everyone has unfavorable circumstances in their lives, but we choose whether we will permit those conditions to rain down on our parade or regard it as an opportunity for further spiritual development.

As for how we feel about the state of our marriages, this type of unhappiness can often stem from feeling like we have an unmet need, which can make us think that we are not receiving our part of the marital bargain.

Because successful Muslim wives are very in tune with their own needs and taking the initiative to be happy, they do not overburden their husbands with trying to fulfill their every desire.

Rather, they create personal happiness by asking:

"What do I need right now to make myself happy?"

It could be that she needs more self-care, or the hanging door fixed, or to see her family more often.

Whatever it may be, a successful Muslim wife taps into her inner self and discovers what she needs in the moment in order to feel better.

If the situation requires it, she may then express that to her husband in a loving way, or if she can achieve it herself, she will do whatever it takes to feel happy again.

> *Maryam was bogged down with taking care of all her young children. She was constantly in 'mom mode' and it was absolutely exhausting.*
>
> *Whenever her husband would return from work, she used this time for venting and complaining about her life – trying to convince him of how hard she had it as a mom.*
>
> *Before having kids, she exercised more and attended Islamic lectures on a regular basis.*

Now she was stuck with the daunting daily tasks of changing diapers, breastfeeding, and restless nights.

Life seemed dismal and what made it worse was that her husband didn't seem to understand what she was going through as a mother, which caused her to secretly blame him for her unhappiness.

After consulting a few friends, some of who were mothers going through a similar experience, she learned that what she really needed was to organize her routine better and schedule in self-care time.

Something as simple as taking a stroll around the block with a baby in the stroller had never occurred to her.

She knew that getting fresh air and seeing greenery would make the world of a difference for her — thus changing her mood.

Depending on another person to make us happy is unrealistic and a sore spot for many women today.

PART 1: MENTAL FOCUS

When we look inside of ourselves for solutions, life becomes easier to live.

When we improve our relationship with ourselves, we gain more confidence and joy. We no longer harbor so much anger towards our husband and blame him for not making the right moves.

WHEN WE LOOK INSIDE OF OURSELVES FOR SOLUTIONS, LIFE BECOMES EASIER TO LIVE. WHEN WE IMPROVE OUR RELATIONSHIP WITH OURSELVES, WE GAIN MORE CONFIDENCE AND JOY.

In summary, what is brewing in our minds will affect the way that we react and respond to our husband. Dwelling on negative thoughts about our husband can become addictive.

Successful Muslim wives actively question their negative thoughts and use them as a guide to understand their husband or their own selves.

They are conscious about what they focus on and challenge harmful thoughts with constructive questions.

So, if being a successful Muslim wife is our mission, then we must realize that we cannot change anything if we do not first change our way of thinking.

Reflection Exercise

Take a moment to reflect about your own life. What do you need right now to be happy and more relaxed in your marriage and home?

_____
_____
_____
_____
_____
_____
_____
_____
_____
_____
_____
_____
_____
_____
_____
_____
_____
_____

PART 2: EMOTIONAL INTELLIGENCE

Three Habits That Define Successful Wives

All too often we trick ourselves into believing that happy marriages are gifted upon the moment that two people agree to marry.

We think that because the two people seem like such a good match together, they will automatically be guaranteed a good relationship.

We might even look at our own marriages and think that if only our husbands were different or if we had married someone who had such-and-such quality, our lives would certainly be better off.

However, forming a good marriage takes a lifetime of consistent effort and work – no matter who you are and what your resume says.

Relationships aren't based upon what we did before we entered them but what we do once we're finally together.

Without a doubt, it's the everyday choices that we make which will mold and define our relationship for the years to come.

Each moment shapes a new day, and each day creates another year, and each following year adds up to a lifetime of bliss or misery.

This mathematical principle applies to every marriage, and none of us can escape how it shapes our destiny – except by learning how to make the right choices so that we gain promising results.

Knowing and understanding which choices are at our fingertips ultimately boils down to our level of emotional intelligence – meaning our ability to effectively analyze our relationship in a way that brings about the most benefit for our minds, hearts, and spirits.

The only thing that will make us become successful wives with blissful marriages is our willingness and aptitude to first consciously opt for the choices that will lead to creating fruitful long-term habits.

A habit is popularly described as a behavior that is repeated regularly until it eventually becomes ingrained at a subconscious level.

This means that the habits we form in our relationships – either good or bad – sooner or later occur without us even thinking about them!

By resorting to their emotional intelligence, successful Muslim wives are acutely aware of how much their personal choices either hurt or help their relationship.

It is their burning desire to always be in the position of guiding the relationship to its greatest potential.

Consequently, successful Muslim wives are extremely selective over which road they will travel during the good and the bad times, and this careful attitude influences them to create three defining habits.

> **HABIT #1: THEY DO NOT REPEAT THE SAME HURTFUL MISTAKES.**

Everyone makes mistakes in their marriages, and certain mistakes may even be repeated a few times before the message finally hits home.

Sometimes the pain that we experience from doing the wrong is what beckons us to try our best the next time.

This bumpy learning process may occur more frequently in the beginning stages of our marriages as we fumble around while trying to get to know our husbands.

Successful Muslim wives are definitely not flawless and they have made their fair share of mistakes, but what separates them from the rest is that they do not repeat the really bad ones.

The Prophet (Allah bless him and give him peace) said, "None of you truly believes until he loves for his brother what he loves for himself." (Bukhari)

Successful Muslim wives want for their husbands what they want for themselves: a tender friendship with their spouse.

Consequently, when these women see how much a specific word, deed, or inaction can rock their marital boat, they consciously choose to take whatever means necessary in order to avoid hurting their husbands.

> *Nadia and her husband had the habit of joking around a lot. Part of their humor involved making fun of each other's faults. It sometimes helped ease the tension between the two during tougher times.*
>
> *One day Nadia's husband forgot to do a task that Nadia had requested from him*

PART 2: EMOTIONAL INTELLIGENCE

the night before. In a sarcastic tone, she critiqued his memory and his capability to follow through with things.

Whereas Nadia was full of laughs, her husband was not as merry. He silently stared back at her with a sad look in his eyes. He then proceeded to carry on with his day as if she didn't exist.

Stunned by her husband giving her the cold shoulder, Nadia inquired about his peculiar behavior.

"I'm just trying my best!" he exclaimed in a loud voice. It was obvious that he felt unfairly criticized and offended by her comment.

Nadia felt extremely guilty about what she had said. Her husband didn't have the best memory when it came to remembering mundane tasks, but he was avid to do what he could to make her happy.

As soon as she realized what happened, she retracted her statement. She told her husband about all of the wonderful things that he had done for her in the past and apologized for her insensitivity.

From that day forward, Nadia trod carefully around making fun of her husband's competence in providing for her needs.

Fundamentally, successful wives are concerned about doing what's right for their marriage and their own lives more than they are about blindly cruising through life, not caring about whom they run over or hit along the way.

SUCCESSFUL WIVES ARE CONCERNED ABOUT DOING WHAT'S RIGHT FOR THEIR MARRIAGE AND THEIR OWN LIVES.

They want to do what is morally and spiritually right for the sake of preserving a good friendship with their husband.

This great habit can plant itself at a deeper level when a wife's love and fear for her Creator serves as the ultimate source of her motivation.

> **HABIT #2: THEY USE CONFLICT AS AN OPPORTUNITY TO DISCOVER AND RECONNECT WITH SHARED VALUES.**

It's become quite popular in today's times to strive for a 'problem-free' life.

Yet, as believers, we are taught that this Life will never be free of tests because this world is not our permanent abode.

Allah Most High says, "He Who created Death and Life, that He may try which of you is best in deed: and He is the Exalted in Might, Oft-Forgiving." (Qur'an 67:2)

Thus, we must view each test as an opportunity to act our best and as an opening to draw nearer to our Creator.

In truth, happiness in this Life does not arise from the absence of problems, but rather it comes from our ability to deal with our problems in a way that is pleasing to Allah Most High.

Every marriage will experience conflict and each couple will dispute about various issues at different times along their marital journey.

However, successful Muslim wives maintain a realistic view about marital life. They appreciate the fact that their marriages may never be argument-free, and instead, they turn their attention to making them argument-friendly.

Instead of allowing fights to break their marital bond, successful Muslim wives treat conflict as an opportunity to connect and learn about each other's needs.

Since their internal drive is wired to further understand their husbands, even if things get heated, the disagreements in these women's marriages will shortly morph into a discussion.

They will find themselves saying curious non-confrontational statements like:

"How come that's so important to you?"

"Why do you think it's best for it to be that way?"

"I totally see the good in what you're saying, but I feel like…"

By squashing their urge to become defensive, insulting, critical, and dismissive over their husband's opinions, they set the stage for their husbands to feel emotionally safe with them.

> *Jawhara was a stay-at-home mom raising a few kids on her own. Her husband's job demanded that he travel for long periods of time away from their family.*
>
> *The couple's main way of communicating with each other was through Skype and email. Yet, the time difference between the countries made it difficult to share what was happening with their kids on a day-to-day basis.*

When he was asleep, she was awake and ready to start her day. When she was winding down for the night, he was charged with energy and curious to find out what the kids were up to that day.

Because her husband was half-way across the globe, Jawhara became stuck with the duty of having to decide what she would allow her kids to do with their schooling and extra-curricular activities.

Sometimes her husband agreed with her choices, while at other times, the two disagreed. These random hiccups often put a strain on the quality of their long-distant relationship.

One day Jawhara found herself in a tight spot. She needed to make a quick decision for one of her kids regarding a school program. In the heat of the moment, she registered.

When Jawhara's husband discovered what she had done, he became irritated. Immediately, she went on the defensive and tried to logically explain her reasoning, but it didn't seem to make matters better.

That night, Jawhara went through a rollercoaster of emotions. She was sick of her husband's nitpickiness. It wasn't easy raising her kids all alone. She just didn't get him. Why was he so upset?

Then it hit her. Maybe he felt left out. He often expressed how hard it was for him to be away from watching his kids grow up. Jawhara's heart softened when she put herself in his shoes.

She decided to write her husband a loving email, explaining why she did what she did and encouraging him to express his concerns.

Her husband responded positively to her openness to hear his side and he even thanked her for all of her hard effort to raise the kids in his absence.

Successful Muslim wives don't busy themselves with trying to prove their point for the sake of being right.

Rather, they welcome their husband's input, acknowledge his view, and encourage him to be vocal for the greater goal of getting along with him.

Each conflict is a prime opportunity to discover something new about their husband and to reconnect with any common values related to life, children, love, and more.

HABIT #3: THEY PRACTICE DAILY GRATITUDE.

Gratitude at its heart means to be thankful for what Allah Most High bestows upon you in your life.

Allah Most High says: "If you are grateful, I will surely increase you." (Qur'an, 14:7)

By showing gratitude to Allah Most High for all of the blessings that He has gifted you, Allah Most High will continue to give you more, especially within your marriage.

The Prophet (Allah bless him and give him peace) said, "Whoever does not thank the people, does not thank Allah." (Tirmidhi)

Successful Muslim wives recognize the gift that gratitude brings to their marriages.

They know that by showing gratitude towards their husbands, they are also thanking Allah Most High in the process, and this will only bring an increase of goodness into their lives.

Showing gratitude also helps successful Muslim wives to focus on the pluses of their relationship and overlook the minuses.

This shift in perspective inspires successful Muslim wives to remember why their husbands are so special – that he is one of their biggest blessings.

> THEY KNOW THAT BY SHOWING GRATITUDE TOWARDS THEIR HUSBANDS, THEY ARE ALSO THANKING ALLAH MOST HIGH IN THE PROCESS.

These wives are not picky either. They are extremely receptive to their husband's kindness and open to accepting whatever good comes their way.

Whether it is that her husband buys her a gift, compliments her cooking, or carries the groceries, a successful Muslim wife accepts her husband's thoughtfulness with delightful satisfaction.

As the years pass and the relationship bond solidifies, it may be that they both develop the habit of showing gratitude for the smallest things that they do for each other.

> *Friends would describe Hafsa as a strong, determined woman who could bulldoze her way through life, getting what she wanted out of people along the way – and her husband was definitely not an excused target.*
>
> *Even though he tried to be patient with her behavior, Hafsa's husband would become frequently annoyed at her way of talking to him. He claimed to feel pressured, bossed around, and controlled by her.*

As the years passed, Hafsa learned that her husband was more motivated by sweet appreciation rather than her overbearing instruction.

She made sure to thank him for any little thing that he did to help her, like serving her a bowl of fruit, filling up the car tank before it ran empty, and making her a cup of coffee in the morning.

With this change in approach, her husband felt increasingly comfortable with doing the things she wanted.

If we keep our eyes open for anything nice that our husband does, even if it's not what we specifically had in mind, it won't seem so difficult to do.

It has been said that a wife's 'thank you' to her husband is the emotional equivalent of him saying 'I love you' to her. In other words, verbal appreciation is super important in a marriage.

It's basic people skills too. When we acknowledge a person for any small act of kindness, they will most likely feel good and want to do more things to please us in the future.

In summary, through their emotional intelligence, successful Muslim wives examine their interactions with their husband.

From their mistakes and triumphs, they LEARN what their husband really desires from them.

They store this knowledge in their emotional database, taking care to update, edit, and save it when required.

Then, this information is used as a reference to mold and shape the good habits in their marriages – for change cannot occur without first knowing what begs to be changed.

Reflection Exercise

Take a moment to reflect about your own husband. What are ten things that you can be grateful for concerning your husband?

_____
_____
_____
_____
_____
_____
_____
_____
_____
_____
_____
_____
_____
_____
_____

PART 3: INTERNAL RESOLVE

THREE COMMITMENTS THAT SUCCESSFUL WIVES MAKE

When we make a commitment, we dedicate ourselves to a worthy cause.

A commitment first originates in the heart as an internal resolve to do something. Thereafter, it is fulfilled and maintained by consistent action.

Just the same, when push comes to shove, blissful marriages are built upon making and keeping strong commitments to perform specific actions.

Successful Muslim wives know this, but they bring a unique twist to this concept.

Instead of fretting about how to carry out more deeds, they put the same amount of emphasis on what actions should <u>not</u> be done.

These ladies steer clear from entering known danger zones, thereby carefully protecting the foundation of their marital bond.

By exercising their personal willpower, they commit themselves towards replacing impulsive harmful reactions with positive counteractions that help increase their husband's love for them.

Commitment #1: They do not dwell on their husband's slip-ups as a father.

Most men are internally wired to be single-focused, meaning that they dedicate their entire attention to completing the task at hand with astounding precision and accuracy. It is a gift that guarantees them success in competitive settings and other areas of their lives.

On the opposite end, most women are internally wired to multitask, which is a skill that can often give them astonishing mastery in domestic settings.

It is no secret that some women feel annoyed at their husband's weakness at not being able to multitask with domestic chores and complete a task as 'perfect' as a woman could.

Some wives may find themselves snapping at their husband's mistakes, especially when it comes to being a father of young children.

Aggravated by his inability to not create an extra mess when feeding the kids, changing the diapers, or playing with the little ones in the backyard, wives in these situations feel that it is their duty to correct and mother their husbands – or to just do everything themselves and forget relying on him.

Successful Muslim wives share the same impulses, but they know that by criticizing their husband's efforts, it will most likely result in discouraging him from taking the initiative to help with the kids in the future.

Because successful Muslim wives strongly desire for their husbands to play the role of an active father, these women take out their magical duct tape, practice patience, and make the moves to demonstrate their happiness for their husband's good-will attempt to help instead.

As one successful Muslim wife described:

> *"When he puts the kids to bed, his goal is to put the baby in the bed and what happens along the way doesn't matter.*
>
> *The baby's clothes may be thrown on the floor, but the baby is definitely in the bed. I talk myself out of commenting. It only takes two seconds to pick up the clothes.*

At the end of the day, he is doing me the favor and I remind myself of that when I feel bothered by his way of doing things."

It's important to note that these wives not only profit from their husband's presence, but their children thrive off of their father's interest in them too.

There is great wisdom in Allah Most High gifting a child with both a father and a mother. Each person possesses traits that will ultimately benefit the child.

Children with dual parental involvement tend to be more focused in school, emotionally sound, and have a better chance at succeeding in life.

Thus, successful Muslim wives make the commitment to not dwell on their husband's blunders, invite him to help, and replace their urge to correct him with an inclination to thank.

By keeping the greater goal in mind, successful Muslim wives motivate their husband to be an involved father through encouraging words and gratitude.

> THERE IS GREAT WISDOM IN ALLAH MOST HIGH GIFTING A CHILD WITH BOTH A FATHER AND A MOTHER. EACH PERSON POSSESSES TRAITS THAT WILL ULTIMATELY BENEFIT THE CHILD.

COMMITMENT #2: THEY DO NOT CROWD THEIR HUSBAND WHEN HE NEEDS SPACE.

It takes a lot of concentration to be single focused.

For this reason, men need alone time to disconnect from their everyday dealings before they can move on to a favorite part of their day: emotionally connecting with their loved ones.

Moreover, when they are trying to solve their own problems related to work, relatives, or finances, they may need an increased amount of alone time.

In an effort to disconnect, a man may engage in watching sports, reading the news, or staring off into the distance – finding comfort in thinking about 'nothing.'

Women are usually the opposite. We need to connect with our loved ones in order to disconnect from our problems and daily routine.

We're innately prepared to socialize, and thinking about 'nothing' is virtually impossible.

Sadly, some wives take their husband's need for space personally. They think that their husband is upset with them when he keeps to himself or voices his need to not be bothered.

These wives may even start asking him, "What's wrong? Are you mad at me?"

When she hears his nonchalant "no" without any affection in return, she assumes that he's too upset to tell her the truth. So, she persists in her inquisition, and he eventually blows up, claiming that he just wants a break.

It could also be that a wife does not intellectually understand her husband's physical need for downtime and space. As a result, she begins to list off all of the things that he could be doing to help make her life easier in those twenty minutes.

When he doesn't budge, she labels him as lazy, irresponsible, and selfish. While she may be looking for him to fulfill a need that she has – hoping that he'll be inspired to multitask while taking his 'break' – little does she realize that if she just gave him that time for space, he would be more charged to help her afterwards.

Successful Muslim wives are no different. They see a man sitting around, not doing anything, and they assume that he has free time on his hands.

However, their experience as a wife has taught them wiser.

Over the years, they have learned to ask if he's available before assigning anymore duties to the sitting duck in their living room.

> *Sophia married her husband while he was still a student. Instead of going to work in*

the morning like most husbands she knew, her husband spent a lot of time at home studying for his classes.

At first, it was exciting to have a stay-at-home husband. But after the couple started to have children, her husband's presence at home became increasingly challenging.

Sophia couldn't help but want to call upon him to join her in anything that she was doing. It was difficult to process that he still needed his own space while he was at home.

Yet, once she stopped taking her husband's need for cave time personally, she grew cheerful again.

She soon realized that she could sit with him in his study room on the odd occasion and just busy herself with doing something quietly.

The Prophet (Allah bless him and give him peace) said, "Verily, the most perfect of believers in faith are those with the best character and who are most kind to their families." (Tirmidhi)

Successful Muslim wives make the commitment to show extra kindness to their husband by understanding his unique needs as a man and giving him the space to fulfill them.

> **COMMITMENT #3: THEY DO NOT HOLD BACK FROM MAKING AMENDS.**

When we are angry at our husbands, the last thing that we want to do is apologize.

This mental block causes us to delay its delivery – convincing ourselves that we're just waiting for the right time, the right words, or the right atmosphere.

Yet, the perfect time never comes and the window to restore peaceful relations eventually closes.

What's crazy is that we change nothing about our method to resolve conflict but expect different results?!

This stalling can also be due to an emotional barrier. Some women are fooled into thinking that making amends will imply weakness, or give the impression that they are giving in on their original position.

It takes a mountain of maturity to overcome such silly excuses!

Successful Muslim wives have climbed up it, pushing themselves every step of the way to repair the connection by way of a simple smile, a friendly touch, or an explicit statement – in spite of simultaneously feeling negative emotions towards their husband.

These women know what treasure apologies bring to their marriages and they have realized that apologizing becomes easier with practice.

> *Amina's husband was recently divorced with kids. Amina had heard bits and pieces about his previous marriage, but she didn't want to bother herself with the gory details. Rather she aimed to start fresh.*

PART 3: INTERNAL RESOLVE

Yet, soon enough, the couple's newlywed stage came to an end and they found themselves squabbling over various issues.

Her husband's way of dealing with conflict was very different from her own. Her husband was more upfront and confrontational, whereas Amina found it easier to be avoidant and give the silent treatment.

Saddened that her marriage was taking a turn for the worse, one day Amina built up the courage to stop ignoring her husband and issue an apology.

Her husband immediately let down his defenses and the two eventually made up with each other. Learning from this experience, Amina made an internal commitment to always apologize for any wrong that she did – knowingly or unknowingly.

Amazingly, her soft apologies often caused her husband to calm down during future disagreements.

> *One day he said to her, "This is the one thing that I never had in my first marriage. She never apologized. MashaAllah, it's why I like being with you. You always apologize."*

Honestly speaking, nothing eases tension, cools burning fury, and heals a wounded heart like a sincere apology, even if the harm was unintentional.

The Prophet (Allah bless him and give him peace) says, "Be merciful to others and you will be shown mercy. Forgive others and Allah will forgive you." (Ahmad)

When push comes to shove, even if we don't want to forgive our husband, we do it out of our commitment to Allah Most High and our commitment to emulate the beautiful character of Prophet (Allah bless him and give him peace).

We must treat others how we want to be treated in this life and the Next. After all, how can we expect Allah Most High to forgive us, when we are not even willing to forgive our husbands?

> WHEN PUSH COMES TO SHOVE, EVEN IF WE DON'T WANT TO FORGIVE OUR HUSBAND, WE DO IT OUT OF OUR COMMITMENT TO ALLAH MOST HIGH AND OUR COMMITMENT TO EMULATE THE BEAUTIFUL CHARACTER OF PROPHET ﷺ.

In conclusion, successful wives are not successful because they always knew the right way.

Quite the contrary, they may have made many mistakes along their marital journey.

Rather, they are winners because they are always working on improving themselves in some shape or form.

By taking steady steps forward, these ladies better their marriages, never giving up despite the challenges that may try to knock them down.

They remain devoted to their internal resolve to make their marriages work for them, and Allah Most High puts blessing in their special secrets.

REFLECTION EXERCISE

Take a moment to reflect about your own heart. What are three things that you are willing to forgive concerning your husband?

_____
_____
_____
_____
_____
_____
_____
_____
_____
_____
_____
_____
_____
_____
_____
_____

ABOUT THE AUTHOR

Naielah Ackbarali is the founder and CEO of Muslima Coaching. She is a trained relationship coach, certified life coach, and a certified NLP Master Practitioner. She has also completed training in the Gottman Method for Couples Therapy.

Combined with her knowledge from Islamic studies, coaching experience, and personal marriage of over 16 years, she offers faith-based marriage coaching for couples, wives, and single sisters. She has helped hundreds of women and couples with almost a decade of coaching experience with clients from all over the world.

Naielah graduated from Florida State University in 2004 with a double major in International Affairs & Sociology. Thereafter, she studied various Islamic sciences with top scholars in both Syria and Jordan for over 15 years. She is currently continuing her advanced Islamic studies in England.

OTHER BOOKS BY NAIELAH ACKBARALI

◆ "Secrets of Successful Muslim Couples: Marriage Tips for a Lifetime" for all spouses.

◆ "Say It With Love: Communicate, Connect & Cure Conflict" for all married sisters.

◆ "Love Scripts: Getting Through To Him" for all married sisters.

◆ "Newlywed Nuggets: Golden Marriage Advice" for newlywed wives.

◆ "A Muslim Woman's Guide To Menstruation Rulings" an intermediate guide for women ages 17+.

◆ "Fiqh of Menstruation Simplified: A Beginner's Guide for Muslim Women" for older teens, beginner learners, and converts.

◆ "Blossom: A Muslim Girl's Period Guide" for girls ages 9 to 14.

◆ "Ramadan Ready: Action Steps for Muslim Women" for older teens and all sisters.

Find them at Kindle or Amazon.
Please rate and review our books!

SIGN UP FOR OUR MARRIAGE COACHING!

MODERN
ISLAMIC ADVICE
Combining the best of both worlds.

AFFORDABLE
PRICES
Half the prices of other professionals.

PRACTICAL
SOLUTIONS
Get realistic advice and set achievable goals.

ONLINE
SESSIONS
Attend sessions in the comfort of your home.

www.muslimacoaching.com
FB: @muslimacoaching IG: @muslima_coaching

Manufactured by Amazon.ca
Acheson, AB